WHAT'S INSIDE....

WIN! L.O.L. SURPRISE GOODIES ON PAGE 40

SNEAK PEAK! LOOK OUT FOR LUXE! FIND THIS ULTRA-RARE CUTIE ON PAGE 77.

MISS BABY

© MGA

OFFICIAL 2018 EDITION

WHO'S IN... GLITTERATI CLUB

WE LOVE ANYTHING THAT GLITTERS!

CRYSTAL QUEEN

DIAMONDS ARE MY BFF

CHARACTER #: 1-001
CLUB: GLITTERATI
RARITY: RARE
SERIES: 1

GLITTER QUEEN

I GLITTERALLY CAN'T!

CHARACTER #: 1-002
CLUB: GLITTERATI
RARITY: RARE
SERIES: 1

SERIES 1

QUEEN BEE

WHAT'S THE BUZZ, HONEY?

CHARACTER #: 1-003
CLUB: GLITTERATI
RARITY: RARE
SERIES: 1

COSMIC QUEEN

WHAT'S YOUR SIGN?

CHARACTER #: 1-004
CLUB: GLITTERATI
RARITY: RARE
SERIES: 1

L.O.L. SURPRISE!

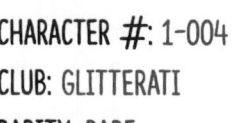

SPLASH QUEEN

I NEED VITAMIN C

CHARACTER #: 2-001

CLUB: GLITTERATI

RARITY: ULTRA-RARE

SERIES: 2

KITTY QUEEN

PURR-FECTION

CHARACTER #: 2-002

CLUB: GLITTERATI

RARITY: RARE

SERIES: 2

SERIES 2

SUGAR QUEEN

NUTS ABOUT THE STAGE!

CHARACTER #: 2-003

CLUB: GLITTERATI

RARITY: RARE

SERIES: 2

THE QUEEN

I'M ALL SHOOK UP!

CHARACTER #: 2-004

CLUB: GLITTERATI

RARITY: RARE

SERIES: 2

LIL SISTERS

LIL GLITTER QUEEN

SERIES 2

"SPARKLE IS LIFE!"

CHARACTER #: 2-037

CLUB: GLITTERATI

RARITY: RARE

SERIES: 2

LIL QUEEN BEE

SERIES 2

"LET'S HANG AT THE HIVE"

CHARACTER #: 2-038

CLUB: GLITTERATI

RARITY: ULTRA-RARE

SERIES: 2

LIL CRYSTAL QUEEN

SERIES 2

"TIARA ON TOP"

CHARACTER #: 2-039

CLUB: GLITTERATI

RARITY: RARE

SERIES: 2

THE LIL QUEEN

SERIES 2

"CRIBHOUSE ROCKER"

CHARACTER #: 2-040

CLUB: GLITTERATI

RARITY: RARE

SERIES: 2

LIL KITTY QUEEN

SERIES 2

"HOW DO U LIKE MEOW?"

CHARACTER #: 2-041

CLUB: GLITTERATI

RARITY: RARE

SERIES: 2

LIL SPLASH QUEEN

SERIES 2

"#FINNING"

CHARACTER #: 2-042

CLUB: GLITTERATI

RARITY: ULTRA-RARE

SERIES: 2

SPARKLING SURPRISE!

MAKE THESE COLOURFUL ICE CUBES WITH HIDDEN GLITTER AND SURPRISE YOUR FRIENDS WITH A DRINK THAT SHIMMERS!

YOU WILL NEED...

- ⭐ A SILICON ICE CUBE TRAY
- ⭐ EDIBLE GLITTER (AVAILABLE FROM CAKE DECORATING SHOPS AND MOST BIG SUPERMARKETS)
- ⭐ WATER
- ⭐ FOOD COLOURING
- ⭐ CLEAR GLASSES
- ⭐ A CLEAR DRINK

L.O.L. SURPRISE!™

HOW TO MAKE IT...

GLITTER ICE CUBES

1. FILL A JUG WITH WATER.

2. ADD A FEW DROPS OF FOOD COLOURING AND LOTS OF EDIBLE GLITTER. STIR WELL.

3. CAREFULLY POUR THE COLOURED WATER INTO AN ICE CUBE TRAY. IF YOU WANT TO MAKE DIFFERENT COLOURED ICE CUBES JUST FILL A SECTION OF THE TRAY THEN REPEAT STEPS 1 AND 2 USING ANOTHER FOOD COLOURING.

4. PLACE THE ICE CUBE TRAY INTO THE FREEZER TO FREEZE OVERNIGHT.

5. PREPARE DRINKS FOR YOUR FRIENDS USING CLEAR GLASSES AND A CLEAR DRINK SUCH AS SPARKLING WATER OR LEMONADE.

6. POP THE ICE CUBES OUT OF THE TRAY AND PUT THEM IN THE DRINKS. AS THE ICE CUBES MELT THEY WILL COLOUR THE DRINK AND RELEASE THE GLITTER!

USE SOME OF YOUR GLITTERY ICE CUBES TO MAKE AN ICE COOL BATH FOR YOUR FAVOURITE COLOUR CHANGE L.O.L. DOLL. POP HER IN THE WATER AND WATCH HER AMAZING COLOUR SURPRISE!

USE A STAR-SHAPED ICE CUBE TRAY TO MAKE YOUR ICE CUBES EVEN MORE EXCITING!

HOLD YOUR DRINK UP TO A BRIGHT LIGHT TO SEE IT AT ITS MOST SPARKLY!

OFFICIAL 2018 EDITION

SURPRISE GIFT BOX

SURPRISE YOUR BFF WITH A THOUGHTFUL GIFT IN A BOX FIT FOR THE GLITTERATI — IT MIGHT BE WHAT'S INSIDE THAT COUNTS BUT THAT DOESN'T MEAN THE OUTSIDE CAN'T BE AMAZING TOO!

HOW TO MAKE

1. FIND AN EMPTY BOX — THE BIGGER THE BETTER.

2. COVER YOUR BOX IN SHINY WRAPPING PAPER AND ADD TONS OF GLITTER.

3. PUT A THOUGHTFUL AND ASTONISHING PRESENT INSIDE — SEE THESE PAGES FOR IDEAS.

4. WATCH YOUR BFF'S FACE LIGHT UP IN WONDER AS SHE OPENS HER GIFT!

© MGA

S

BEAUTIFUL BALLOON

PLACE A HELIUM BALLOON IN THE BOX SO THAT WHEN YOUR FRIEND OPENS IT, THE BALLOON FLOATS OUT!

LOTS OF BOXES

DECORATE LOTS OF DIFFERENT SIZED BOXES AND PUT A PRESENT INSIDE THE SMALLEST ONE. PUT THE SMALL BOX INSIDE A BIGGER BOX AND SO ON UNTIL YOU ARE LEFT WITH JUST ONE HUGE BOX. YOUR FRIEND CERTAINLY WON'T BE EXPECTING TO FIND THAT WHEN SHE OPENS HER GIFT!

LUCKY DIP

MAKE YOUR FRIEND HER OWN LUCKY DIP BY WRAPPING UP LOTS OF LITTLE PRESENTS, FILLING YOUR BOX WITH POLYSTYRENE SHAPES AND HIDING THE GIFTS INSIDE. SHE'LL LOVE THE SURPRISE OF DISCOVERING WHAT'S INSIDE EACH PRETTY PACKAGE.

COLOURFUL GIFT

DECORATE THE BOX IN YOUR FRIEND'S FAVOURITE COLOUR AND FILL IT WITH GIFTS OF THE SAME COLOUR. SHE'LL LOVE HER BIG BOX OF PINK (OR BLUE, OR PURPLE, OR RED...)!

WHO'S IN... OPPOSITES CLUB

WE LOVE TO BE DIFFERENT!

FANCY

MORE ISSUES THAN CHIC MAGAZINE

CHARACTER #: 1-005

CLUB: OPPOSITES

RARITY: POPULAR

SERIES: 1

SERIES 1

FRESH

CHILL OUT AND UNSUBSCRIBE

CHARACTER #: 1-006

CLUB: OPPOSITES

RARITY: POPULAR

SERIES: 1

BEING DIFFERENT MAKES OUR WORLD GO AROUND

SUGAR

SWEET AS CANDY!

SERIES 2

CHARACTER #: 2-006
CLUB: OPPOSITES
RARITY: FANCY
SERIES: 2

SPICE

HOT LIKE A PEPPER!

CHARACTER #: 2-007
CLUB: OPPOSITES
RARITY: POPULAR
SERIES: 2

LIL SISTERS

LIL FRESH

SERIES 2

"MY STYLE NEVER EXPIRES"
CHARACTER #: 2-045
CLUB: OPPOSITES
RARITY: POPULAR
SERIES: 2

LIL FANCY

SERIES 2

"ALWAYS LOOK YOUR BEST"
CHARACTER #: 2-046
CLUB: OPPOSITES
RARITY: POPULAR
SERIES: 2

LIL SUGAR

SERIES 2

"AGREE TO DISAGREE!"
CHARACTER #: 2-047
CLUB: OPPOSITES
RARITY: ULTRA-RARE
SERIES: 2

LIL SPICE

SERIES 2

"YOU'RE WRONG; I'M RIGHT!"
CHARACTER #: 2-048
CLUB: OPPOSITES
RARITY: ULTRA-RARE
SERIES: 2

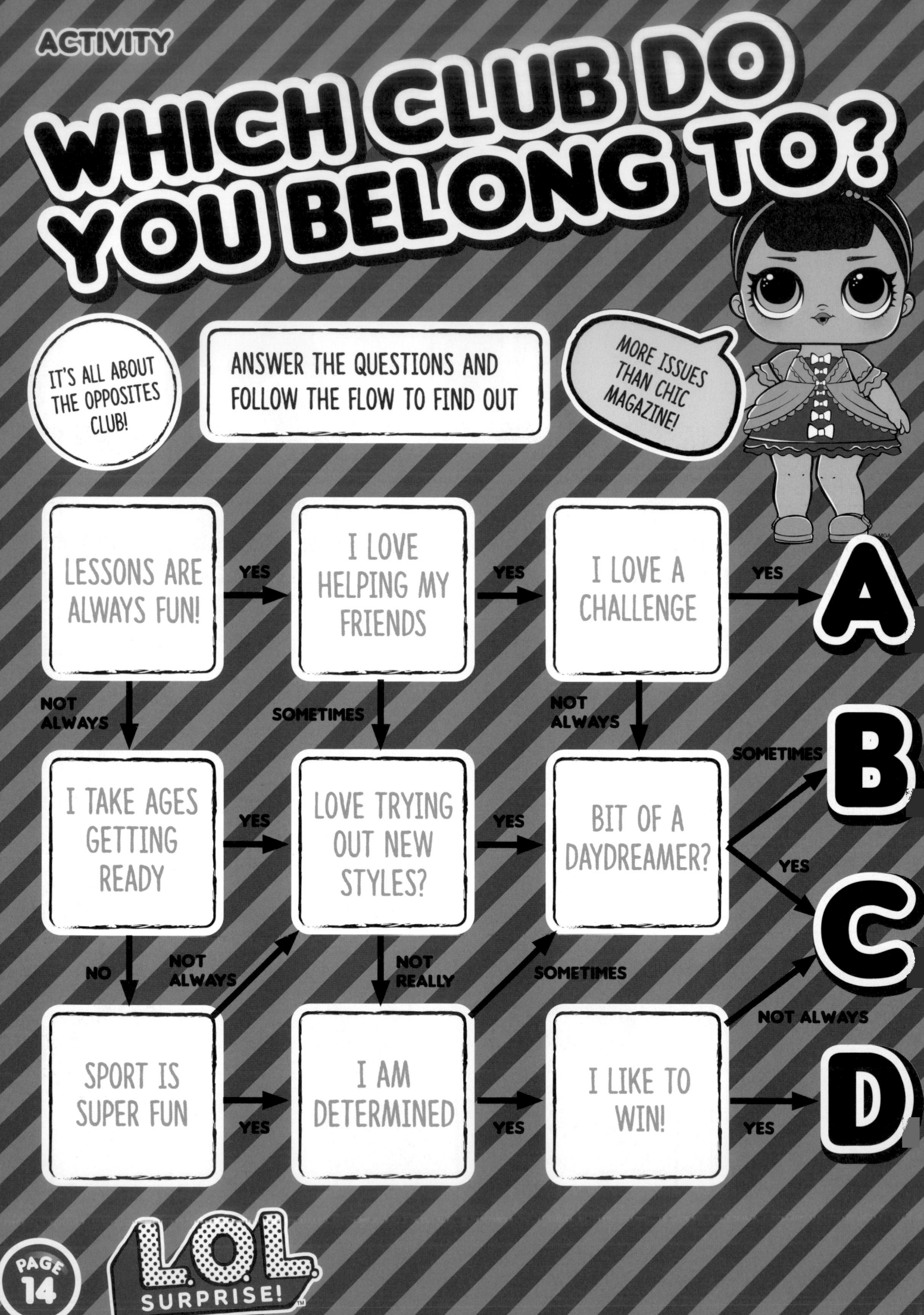

YOU'RE IN...
SPIRIT CLUB!

YOU'RE A HAPPY, CONFIDENT AND BUBBLY FRIEND WHO'S ALWAYS LOOKING FOR THE NEXT FUN ADVENTURE!

YOU'RE IN...
GLAM CLUB!

YOU LOVE HAVING FUN WITH FASHION, CUSTOMISING YOUR CLOTHES AND GIVING YOUR FRIENDS MAKEOVERS.

WHICH CLUB IS FOR YOU?

YOU'RE IN...
THEATER CLUB

YOU CAN BE A BIT OF A DAYDREAMER AND LOVE MAKE-BELIEVE, BUT THAT JUST MAKES YOU THE FUN-EST FRIEND TO BE AROUND.

YOU'RE IN...
ATHLETIC CLUB

YOU LOVE PLAYING SPORT AND HAVE BAGS ON ENERGY. YOUR FRIENDS LOVE BEING AROUND YOU, AS LONG AS YOU CAN SIT STILL FOR FIVE MINUTES!

WHO'S IN... GLEE CLUB

WE'VE GOT SWAGGER!

ROCKER

I ROCKED B4 I COULD WALK

CHARACTER #: 1-011
CLUB: GLEE
RARITY: POPULAR
SERIES: 1

SERIES 1

DIVA

BORN THIS WAY!

CHARACTER #: 1-012
CLUB: GLEE
RARITY: FANCY
SERIES: 1

M.C. SWAG

PASS ME THE MIC

CHARACTER #: 1-013
CLUB: GLEE
RARITY: POPULAR
SERIES: 1

L.O.L. SURPRISE!

LIL M.C. SWAG

PARTYING IS IN OUR DNA!

"SPITTIN' RHYMES B4 NAPTIME!"

CHARACTER #: 1-014

CLUB: GLEE

RARITY: ULTRA-RARE

SERIES: 1

LIL SISTERS

LIL ROCKER

"ROCK ON"

CHARACTER #: 2-049

CLUB: GLEE

RARITY: POPULAR

SERIES: 2

SERIES 2

LIL DIVA

"SLAY ALL DAY!"

CHARACTER #: 2-050

CLUB: GLEE

RARITY: FANCY

SERIES: 2

SCHOOL OF ROCK!

GET YOUR FRIENDS TOGETHER TO FORM THE ULTIMATE ROCK BAND!

BAND NAME

USE ROCKER'S BAND-NAME GENERATOR TO DISCOVER YOUR BAND'S NAME!

NEED A SICK DANCE ROUTINE TO GO WITH YOUR SONG? TURN TO PAGE 38 TO FIND OUT HOW!

WHAT DAY OF THE WEEK IS IT?

MON - TUE	THE DAZZLING
WED - THURS	THE LOUD
FRI - SAT - SUN	THE ROCKING

WHAT'S THE WEATHER LIKE?

SUNNY	DIAMONDS
RAIN / SNOW	KITTENS
CLOUDY	SUPERSTARS

L.O.L. SURPRISE!

WHAT'S YOUR ROLE?

MAKE A BAND

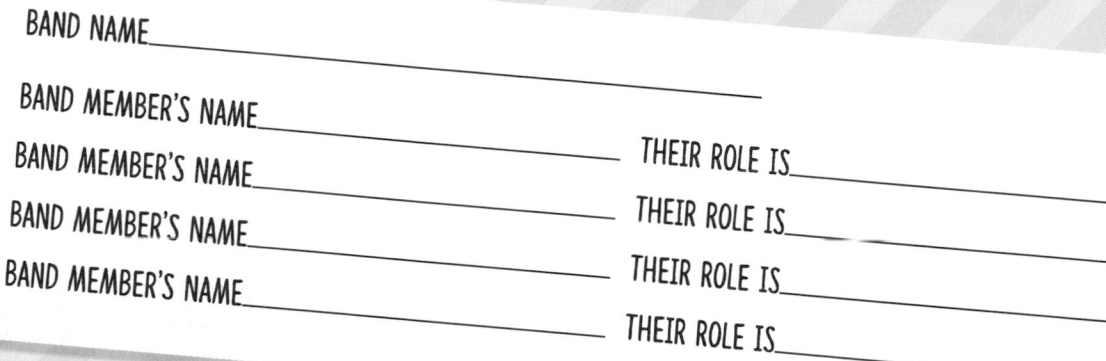

I ROCKED 'TIL I COULD WALK!

TIME TO GIVE YOU AND YOUR FRIENDS THEIR ROLE IN THE BAND. IF ANY OF YOU PLAY AN INSTRUMENT, GREAT! IF YOU DON'T, YOU COULD JUST BE A SINGING GROUP (LIKE LITTLE MIX) OR YOU COULD EVEN PRETEND TO PLAY INSTRUMENTS. IF YOU DON'T FANCY PERFORMING, YOU COULD BE THE BAND MANAGER INSTEAD. WHEN YOU HAVE YOUR ROLES, FILL THEM OUT!

ROCK ON!

BAND NAME_____

BAND MEMBER'S NAME_____

BAND MEMBER'S NAME_____ THEIR ROLE IS_____

BAND MEMBER'S NAME_____ THEIR ROLE IS_____

BAND MEMBER'S NAME_____ THEIR ROLE IS_____

THEIR ROLE IS_____

READY TO ROCK, OR TOTALLY CHILLED OUT?

YOU'VE GOT YOUR NAME, YOU'VE GOT YOUR FRIENDS, NOW WHAT ABOUT THE MUSIC? YOU COULD CHOOSE YOUR FAVOURITE SONGS AND DO A 'COVER' (THIS MEANS SINGING A SONG THAT'S ALREADY BEEN WRITTEN) OR YOU COULD MAKE ONE UP YOURSELF.

ALBUM COVER

USE THE SPACE HERE TO DESIGN YOUR FIRST ALBUM COVER. YOU COULD DRAW A PICTURE OF YOU AND YOUR FRIENDS, OR YOU COULD COME UP WITH A TOTALLY UNIQUE DESIGN!

OFFICIAL 2018 EDITION

WHO'S IN... ATHLETIC CLUB

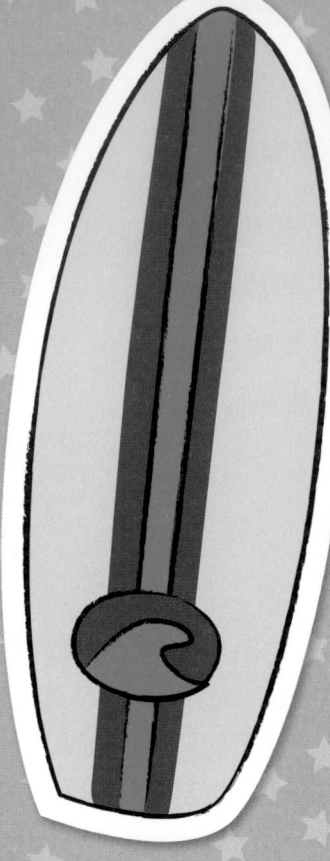

SURFER BABE

> 4 SHORE

CHARACTER #: 1-018
CLUB: ATHLETIC
RARITY: POPULAR
SERIES: 1

> WE LOVE TO CATCH SOME WAVES!

SERIES 1

HOOPS MVP

> DRIBBLE, DRIBBLE, SCORE!

CHARACTER #: 1-019
CLUB: ATHLETIC
RARITY: POPULAR
SERIES: 1

ROLLER SK8ER

> SK8, DON'T HATE!

CHARACTER #: 1-020
CLUB: ATHLETIC
RARITY: FANCY
SERIES: 1

KEEP UP WITH US IF YOU CAN!

4 SHORE

ICE SK8ER

QUEEN OF THE RINK

CHARACTER #: 2-011
CLUB: ATHLETIC
RARITY: FANCY
SERIES: 2

SERIES 2

KICKS

GOOOOOOO-OOOOAL!

CHARACTER #: 2-012
CLUB: ATHLETIC
RARITY: POPULAR
SERIES: 2

COURT CHAMP

I GOT GAME!

CHARACTER #: 2-013
CLUB: ATHLETIC
RARITY: POPULAR
SERIES: 2

SK8

LIL SISTERS

LIL ROLLER SK8ER

SERIES 1

"THAT'S HOW I ROLL!"

CHARACTER #: 1-021
CLUB: ATHLETIC
RARITY: ULTRA-RARE
SERIES: 1

LIL HOOPS MVP

SERIES 2

"IN IT TO WIN IT!"

CHARACTER #: 2-051
CLUB: ATHLETIC
RARITY: POPULAR
SERIES: 2

LIL SURFER BABE

SERIES 2

"BEACH IS MY BAE"

CHARACTER #: 2-052
CLUB: ATHLETIC
RARITY: POPULAR
SERIES: 2

LIL ICE SK8ER

SERIES 2

"YOU'RE ON THIN ICE!"

CHARACTER #: 2-053
CLUB: ATHLETIC
RARITY: FANCY
SERIES: 2

LIL KICKS

SERIES 2

"SCORE!"

CHARACTER #: 2-054
CLUB: ATHLETIC
RARITY: POPULAR
SERIES: 2

ON YOUR MARKS!

WHO SAYS SPORTS DAYS ARE JUST FOR SCHOOL?

YOUR VENUE

IF IT'S A NICE DAY, YOUR GARDEN OR LOCAL PARK ARE PERFECT FOR SPORTS. ANYWHERE THERE IS A PATCH OF SOFT GROUND LIKE GRASS.

THE GAMES!

EGG AND SPOON

YOU WILL NEED:
- TABLESPOONS
- BOILED EGGS (WITH THE SHELLS STILL ON)
- A WHISTLE.

THE AIM OF THIS GAME IS TO BE THE FIRST TO CROSS THE FINISH LINE WHILE CARRYING YOUR BOILED EGG ON A SPOON! GIVE EACH PLAYER A TABLESPOON AND PLACE AN EGG ON TOP. MARK OUT THE START AND END OF THE RACE, BEFORE BLOWING A WHISTLE TO BEGIN.

DRIBBLE, DRIBBLE, SCORE!

© MGA

THREE-LEGGED RACE

YOU WILL NEED:
- A COUPLE OF SCARVES

WORK TOGETHER WITH A FRIEND TO BE THE SPEEDIEST PAIR IN THE RACE. DIVIDE INTO PAIRS THEN STAND SIDE BY SIDE WITH YOUR PARTNER. USE A SCARF TO TIE ONE OF EACH OF YOUR LEGS TOGETHER, THEN WHEN THE WHISTLE BLOWS, RUN AS FAST AS YOU CAN TO THE FINISH LINE!

BEAN BAG TOSS

YOU WILL NEED:

SMALL BEAN BAGS
A RULER
PENCILS

BE THE ONE WHO THROWS THE FURTHEST! MARK A SPOT ON THE GRASS WITH A RULER, THEN TAKE IT IN TURNS TO THROW A BEAN BAG WHILE STANDING BEHIND THE RULER. PLACE A PENCIL ON THE GROUND TO MARK WHERE EACH PLAYER'S BEAN BAG LANDED. WHOEVER THROWS THE FURTHEST IS THE WINNER.

SPORTS DAY

GOOOOOOO-OOOOAL!

LONG JUMP

YOU WILL NEED:

A RULER
PENCILS
A LONG STRIP OF GRASS

MARK A SPOT IN THE GROUND WITH A RULER. ALL PLAYERS MUST STAND BEHIND THE RULER BEFORE JUMPING. BEND YOUR KNEES AND SEE HOW FAR YOU CAN JUMP FROM THAT SPOT. MARK THE LENGTH OF EACH JUMP WITH A PENCIL. WHOEVER JUMPS THE FURTHEST IS THE WINNER.

DESIGN YOUR MEDALS

PHOTOCOPY THE TEMPLATE BELOW TO DESIGN A MEDAL FOR FIRST, SECOND AND THIRD PLACE. YOU COULD EVEN MAKE A TROPHY FOR THE PERSON WHO WINS THE MOST EVENTS!

CAN YOU THINK OF ANY MORE FUN SPORTS?

WATER FUN!

SURFER BABE LOVES HANGING OUT BY THE WATER! READ ON TO DISCOVER SOME OF HER FAVE BEACH AND WATER GAMES AND LEARN SOME TOP TIPS FOR STAYING SAFE.

WARNING!

ALWAYS TAKE EXTRA CARE WHEN PLAYING IN OR NEAR WATER.

STONE TOWERS

COLLECT PEBBLES FROM THE BEACH AND USE THEM TO BUILD TOWERS. WHOEVER BUILDS THE HIGHEST TOWER IS THE WINNER. IF YOU WANT TO MAKE THE GAME MORE EXCITING PLAY AGAINST THE CLOCK AND WORK IN TEAMS TO BUILD A TOWER IN JUST ONE MINUTE!

BEACH BATH

DIG A BATH IN THE SAND BIG ENOUGH FOR YOUR L.O.L. DOLL TO FIT IN. LINE THE BATH WITH PEBBLES, SHELLS OR ANYTHING ELSE YOU CAN FIND ON THE BEACH WHICH WILL HELP TO STOP THE BATH WATER SOAKING INTO THE SAND. WHEN EVERYONE'S BATH IS READY FILL THEM WITH THE SAME AMOUNT OF WATER. WHOEVER'S BATH HOLDS THE WATER THE LONGEST IS THE WINNER!

WATER RELAY

DIVIDE YOUR FRIENDS INTO TWO TEAMS. GIVE EACH TEAM A BUCKET AND A PLASTIC CUP. TAKE IT IN TURNS TO RACE TO A LARGE BOWL OR POOL OF WATER, FILL THE CUP, RUN BACK TO THE BUCKET AND EMPTY THE WATER INTO IT. THE FIRST TEAM TO FILL ITS BUCKET IS THE WINNER. IF YOU DON'T HAVE PLASTIC CUPS OR WANT TO MAKE THE RELAY EVEN TRICKIER YOU COULD USE YOUR HANDS TO COLLECT THE WATER!

SAND PORTRAITS

COLLECT ITEMS FROM THE BEACH SUCH AS SHELLS AND PEBBLES AND USE THEM TO CREATE A PICTURE OF ONE OF YOUR FRIENDS OR YOUR FAVOURITE L.O.L. DOLL. WHEN EVERYONE HAS FINISHED TAKE TURNS TO GUESS WHO EACH PORTRAIT IS OF.

FLOAT OR SINK?

COLLECT A VARIETY OF HOUSEHOLD OBJECTS OF DIFFERENT SIZES AND SHAPES SUCH AS DRIED PASTA, A BAR OF SOAP, A PENCIL, A PLASTIC SPOON AND A PIECE OF CARDBOARD. FILL A LARGE BOWL WITH WATER AND GUESS WHETHER EACH OBJECT WILL FLOAT OR SINK. PLACE THE ITEMS IN THE WATER TO SEE IF YOU WERE RIGHT!

4 SHORE

BEACH IS MY BAE

© MGA

WATER TAG

GIVE A WATER SQUIRTER FILLED WITH WATER TO ONE PLAYER — THEY ARE 'IT'. ALL THE OTHER PLAYERS HAVE TO RUN AWAY WHILE IT TRIES TO TAG THEM WITH A SQUIRT OF WATER. ONCE A PLAYER HAS BEEN HIT THEY'RE OUT OF THE GAME. THE WINNER IS THE LAST PERSON TO BE SQUIRTED. YOU CAN PLAY THIS GAME OVER AND OVER AGAIN, TAKING IT IN TURNS TO BE IT.

BEACH AND WATER SAFETY

⭐ ALWAYS SWIM WITH A PARTNER. DON'T GO INTO THE WATER ALONE.

⭐ KNOW YOUR LIMITS. IF YOU'RE NOT A STRONG SWIMMER DON'T GO OUT OF YOUR DEPTH.

⭐ ONLY JUMP OR DIVE INTO WATER IN AREAS THAT ARE KNOWN TO BE SAFE. CHECK HOW DEEP THE WATER IS BEFORE YOU JUMP AND MAKE SURE THERE AREN'T ANY HIDDEN ROCKS OR OTHER HAZARDS BENEATH THE SURFACE.

⭐ AT THE BEACH, MAKE SURE YOU KNOW WHEN THE TIDE IS DUE TO COME IN SO YOU DON'T ACCIDENTALLY GET CUT OFF.

⭐ BEFORE YOU GO IN THE SEA CHECK TO SEE IF THERE ARE ANY FLAGS OR SIGNS WARNING OF WATER DANGERS. IF YOU SEE A RED FLAG FLYING IT MEANS DANGER SO DON'T GO IN THE WATER UNDER ANY CIRCUMSTANCES.

⭐ DON'T USE INFLATABLES IN THE SEA IF IT'S WINDY OR THE WAVES ARE BIG — THEY'RE DESIGNED FOR SWIMMING POOLS AND CAN EASILY BE SWEPT AWAY.

⭐ IF YOU SEE SOMEBODY IN DANGER IN THE WATER TELL A LIFEGUARD STRAIGHT AWAY. IF THERE ISN'T A LIFEGUARD TELL AN ADULT.

OFFICIAL 2018 EDITION

WHO'S IN... THEATER CLUB

WE CAN BE ANYTHING WE WANT!

MERBABY

I'D RATHER BE SWIMMING

CHARACTER #: 1-015
CLUB: THEATER
RARITY: POPULAR
SERIES: 1

SERIES 1

BABY CAT

CHECK MEOWT

CHARACTER #: 1-016
CLUB: THEATER
RARITY: POPULAR
SERIES: 1

SUPER B.B.

SAVING THE WORLD B4 BEDTIME

CHARACTER #: 1-017
CLUB: THEATER
RARITY: FANCY
SERIES: 1

L.O.L. SURPRISE!™

GENIE

YOU WISH!

CHARACTER #: 2-008
CLUB: THEATER
RARITY: FANCY
SERIES: 2

TODAY, WE ARE SUPERHEROES. TOMORROW, WHO KNOWS!

SERIES 2

PRANKSTA

LOL JK

CHARACTER #: 2-009
CLUB: THEATER
RARITY: POPULAR
SERIES: 2

COCONUT Q.T.

YOU HAD ME AT ALOHA!

CHARACTER #: 2-010
CLUB: THEATER
RARITY: POPULAR
SERIES: 2

LIL SISTERS

LIL MERBABY

SERIES 2

"CATCH ME BY THE SEA"

CHARACTER #: 2-055
CLUB: THEATER
RARITY: POPULAR
SERIES: 2

LIL BABY CAT

SERIES 2

"STAY PAW-SITIVE"

CHARACTER #: 2-056
CLUB: THEATER
RARITY: POPULAR
SERIES: 2

LIL GENIE

SERIES 2

"IN YOUR DREAMS!"

CHARACTER #: 2-057
CLUB: THEATER
RARITY: FANCY
SERIES: 2

OFFICIAL 2018 EDITION

ACT IT OUT!

BECOME HONORARY MEMBERS OF THE THEATER CLUB AND WRITE AND PERFORM AN L.O.L. SPACE-THEMED PLAY FOR YOUR FRIENDS AND FAMILY TO WATCH! HERE'S HOW...

THE STORY OUTLINE

IN A WORLD WHERE BABIES RUN EVERYTHING, MERBABY, BABY CAT AND SUPER B.B. CAN BE ANYTHING THEY WANT TO BE. ONE DAY THEY DECIDE TO MAKE HISTORY BY BECOMING THE FIRST BABIES TO FLY INTO SPACE! THEY ARE SURE TO HAVE LOTS OF ADVENTURES ALONG THE WAY CUZ IN THIS WORLD NOTHING IT DULL – IT'S ALL A LIL' SURPRISING AND OUTRAGEOUS!

WRITE A SCRIPT

USE THE STORY OUTLINE ABOVE TO CREATE YOUR STORY AND WRITE YOUR SCRIPT. THE SCRIPT SHOULD SET THE SCENE AND GIVE THE CHARACTERS THEIR LINES. FOR EXAMPLE:

[MERBABY, BABY CAT AND SUPER B.B. ARE BOARDING THEIR ROCKET TO FLY INTO SPACE FOR THE VERY FIRST TIME. THEY ARE JUMPING ABOUT WITH EXCITEMENT]

MERBABY: I CAN'T BELIEVE WE'RE ACTUALLY GONNA DO THIS!

SUPER B.B.: I KNOW! THIS IS THE BEST THING EVER!

BABY CAT: WHAT DO YOU THINK WE'LL FIND UP THERE?

SUPER B.B.: ALIENS! PLEASE LET IT BE ALIENS!

PRACTISE!

PRACTISE YOUR PLAY UNTIL EVERYONE REMEMBERS THEIR LINES AND FEELS COMFORTABLE ON STAGE. DON'T FORGET TO HAVE A DRESS REHEARSAL SO WHEN IT COMES TO THE REAL PERFORMANCE YOUR CAST WILL BE PREPARED.

PICK A CAST

CHOOSE WHO WILL PERFORM IN YOUR PLAY. YOU COULD ASK SOME FRIENDS AND DECIDE TOGETHER WHO WILL PLAY WHICH PART. IF YOU WANT TO PERFORM THE PLAY ON YOUR OWN WHY NOT USE TEDDIES AS THE OTHER CHARACTERS?

CHOOSE YOUR STAGE

WHERE WILL YOU PERFORM YOUR PLAY? YOU NEED SPACE FOR A STAGE (THIS DOESN'T HAVE TO BE A RAISED PLATFORM, JUST AN OPEN SPACE WHERE THE CAST HAVE ROOM TO MOVE) AND A PLACE FOR YOUR AUDIENCE TO SIT. YOU COULD SET OUT CHAIRS OR JUST PUT CUSHIONS ON THE FLOOR. IF IT'S A NICE DAY YOU COULD PERFORM YOUR PLAY IN THE GARDEN OR AT A PARK.

BUILD YOUR SET

A SET WILL HELP BRING YOUR PLAY TO LIFE. IT CAN BE AS ELABORATE OR SIMPLE AS YOU LIKE. YOU COULD PAINT A BACKDROP OF A STARRY SKY AND PLANETS ONTO AN OLD SHEET AND HANG IT UP BEHIND THE STAGE OR MAKE A SPACE ROCKET OUT OF CARDBOARD BOXES.

MAKE YOUR COSTUMES

DRESSING UP IN COSTUME IS ONE OF THE BEST THINGS ABOUT PUTTING ON A PLAY! HAVE A LOOK THROUGH YOUR WARDROBE FOR ANYTHING THAT IS SUITABLE OR MAKE SIMPLE COSTUMES FROM STUFF YOU FIND AROUND THE HOUSE. ANYTHING WHITE OR SILVER CAN BE USED TO MAKE A SPACESUIT AND YOU COULD MAKE HELMETS OUT OF CARDBOARD BOXES COVERED IN TINFOIL WITH A HOLE CUT OUT FOR YOUR FACE.

TIMESAVER!
IF YOU DON'T HAVE TIME TO WRITE A PLAY WHY NOT IMPROVISE? THIS MEANS YOU MAKE IT UP AS YOU GO ALONG! IMPROVISED PLAYS ARE A SURPRISE FOR BOTH THE AUDIENCE AND THE CAST!

FIGHT THE STAGE FRIGHT! IT'S TOTALLY NORMAL TO FEEL A BIT NERVOUS BEFORE GOING ON STAGE. TAKE A FEW DEEP BREATHS TO CALM ANY NERVES AND ONCE YOU'RE ON JUST GO FOR IT AND HAVE FUN!

ADD SOME MUSIC

DOES YOUR PLAY NEED MUSIC? IF SO, MAKE SURE YOU HAVE ALL THE SONGS IN ONE PLACE AND SOMETHING YOU CAN PLAY THEM THROUGH. IF YOU LOVE SINGING YOU COULD MAKE YOUR PLAY A MUSICAL WHERE ALL THE WORDS ARE SUNG INSTEAD OF SPOKEN! AND IF YOU WANT TO INCLUDE DANCE ROUTINES REMEMBER, PRACTISE MAKES PERFECT!

WHO'S IN...
SPIRIT CLUB

" ...GIVE ME AN S. P. I. R. I. T. "

MAJORETTE

FOLLOW MY LEAD!

CHARACTER #: 1-007
CLUB: SPIRIT
RARITY: FANCY
SERIES: 1

SERIES 1

TEACHER'S PET

STRAIGHT A'S 4 EVA

CHARACTER #: 1-008
CLUB: SPIRIT
RARITY: POPULAR
SERIES: 1

CHEER CAPTAIN

TEAMWORK MAKES THE DREAMWORK!

CHARACTER #: 1-009
CLUB: SPIRIT
RARITY: POPULAR
SERIES: 1

IT'S HARD BEING THIS CLEVER!

SERIES 1

LIL CHEER CAPTAIN

"GAGA FOR RA-RA!"

CHARACTER #: 1-010

CLUB: SPIRIT

RARITY: ULTRA-RARE

SERIES: 1

LIL SISTERS

LIL MAJORETTE

"LET'S GET IN FORMATION"

CHARACTER #: 2-043

CLUB: SPIRIT

RARITY: FANCY

SERIES: 2

SERIES 2

LIL TEACHER'S PET

"YOU'RE NEVER TOO YOUNG TO LEARN!"

CHARACTER #: 2-044

CLUB: SPIRIT

RARITY: POPULAR

SERIES: 2

CREATE AN UNBOXING VIDEO

UNBOXING VIDEOS HAVE BECOME MORE SUCCESSFUL THAN ANYONE COULD EVER HAVE IMAGINED. FOLLOW OUR SIMPLE STEPS TO BECOMING AN UNBOXING SENSATION!

WHAT IS AN UNBOXER?

AN UNBOXER IS SOMEONE WHO FILMS THEMSELVES UNPACKING NEW TOYS OR GADGETS. THEY THEN UPLOAD THE FILM ONTO A VIDEO SHARING PLATFORM SUCH AS YOUTUBE FOR ANYONE, ANYWHERE IN THE WORLD TO SEE. THE MOST SUCCESSFUL UNBOXERS HAVE MILLIONS OF FOLLOWERS AROUND THE WORLD.

S

HOW TO UNBOX LIKE A PRO

1 CHOOSE THE RIGHT PRODUCT YOU NEED TO FIND A TOY OR GADGET THAT PEOPLE WILL LOVE. THE MORE BITS THERE ARE TO THE PACKAGE THE MORE INTERESTING IT WILL BE FOR YOUR VIEWERS TO WATCH – THAT'S WHAT MAKES L.O.L. DOLLS THE PERFECT TOY TO UNBOX!

2 PREPARE THE BOX CUT ANY TAPE THAT'S HOLDING THE BOX SHUT BEFORE YOU START FILMING TO MAKE IT EASIER TO OPEN SMOOTHLY. AND KEEP YOUR SCISSORS CLOSE BY IN CASE THE INSIDE PACKAGING IS TRICKY TO GET INTO!

3 KEEP THE QUALITY HIGH WHEN YOU'RE FILMING THINK ABOUT LIGHTING, SOUND AND PICTURE QUALITY. YOU WANT YOUR VIDEO TO LOOK AS PROFESSIONAL AS POSSIBLE. USE A TRIPOD TO MAKE SURE YOUR VIDEO IS STABLE WITH NO JERKS OR WOBBLES. IF YOU DON'T HAVE A TRIPOD REST YOUR PHONE OR TABLET ON A FLAT, SOLID SURFACE SUCH AS A TABLE OR SHELF AND PROP IT UP WITH A HEAVY BOOK TO STOP IT SLIDING. MAKE SURE THE BOOK ISN'T OBSCURING THE CAMERA LENS.

4 SET THE SCENE BEFORE YOU BEGIN TO OPEN THE BOX TELL YOUR AUDIENCE A LITTLE BIT ABOUT THE PRODUCT SO THAT THEY KNOW EXACTLY WHAT THEY'RE ABOUT TO SEE. TELL THEM WHERE YOU BOUGHT IT AND HOW MUCH IT COST. BUT KEEP YOUR INTRO SHORT AND OPEN THE BOX EARLY ON IN YOUR MOVIE – THAT'S WHAT EVERYONE WANTS TO SEE, AFTER ALL!

5 BE YOURSELF TRY TO TALK NATURALLY AND DON'T WORRY IF YOU MAKE A MISTAKE. THE BEST UNBOXING VIDEOS ARE LIGHT-HEARTED WITH A LITTLE BIT OF HUMOUR THROWN IN. BE YOURSELF AND LET YOUR PERSONALITY SHINE THROUGH.

6 SAY WHAT YOU SEE DESCRIBE EXACTLY WHAT'S INSIDE YOUR BOX AS YOU OPEN IT. WHAT ARE THE ITEMS? WHAT DO YOU DO WITH THEM? DO YOU LIKE THEM? FINISH YOUR VIDEO WITH A CLOSE-UP SHOT OF THE ASSEMBLED PRODUCT.

7 STAND OUT FROM THE CROWD COME UP WITH A GREAT TITLE FOR YOUR UNBOXING VIDEO AND ADD AN EYE-CATCHING THUMBNAIL TO MAKE SURE YOU GET NOTICED.

8 SPREAD THE WORD AT THE END OF YOUR FILM INVITE YOUR VIEWERS TO SUBSCRIBE TO YOUR CHANNEL AND ASK YOUR FRIENDS AND FAMILY TO SHARE YOUR VIDEO THROUGH PLATFORMS SUCH AS TWITTER AND FACEBOOK. THE MORE NOISE YOU MAKE ABOUT YOUR VIDEO THE MORE VIEWS IT WILL GET. IN THE WORLD OF UNBOXING, IT'S ALL ABOUT THE NUMBERS!

WARNING!

ALWAYS GET PERMISSION FROM A PARENT OR CARER BEFORE UPLOADING ANYTHING ONTO THE INTERNET.

SECRET CODE

WANT TO CREATE A SECRET LANGUAGE CODE THAT ONLY YOUR CLUB CAN UNDERSTAND? HERE'S HOW...

A B C D E F G

H I J K L

M N O P Q

R S T U V

W X Y Z

1. JOIN TOGETHER WITH A FEW FRIENDS TO MAKE A CLUB. DECIDE WHAT YOUR CLUB THEME WILL BE AND CHOOSE A COOL NAME.

2. NOW THAT YOU HAVE YOUR CLUB, YOU NEED A SECRET LANGUAGE SO YOU CAN SEND EACH OTHER MESSAGES THAT NOBODY ELSE WILL BE ABLE TO READ. CHOOSE A LETTER, NUMBER OR SYMBOL TO REPRESENT EACH LETTER OF THE ALPHABET AND WRITE OR DRAW THEM ONTO THE GRID ON THE LEFT.

3. PHOTOCOPY THE ALPHABET GRID AND GIVE ONE TO EACH MEMBER OF YOUR CLUB. MAKE SURE NOBODY ELSE CAN GET HOLD OF A COPY! IF YOU DON'T HAVE ACCESS TO A PHOTOCOPIER EACH CLUB MEMBER CAN COPY THE GRID BY HAND.

4. WRITE SECRET MESSAGES TO EACH OTHER AND USE THE GRID TO DECIPHER WHAT THEY SAY!

SUPER TOP SECRET

HOW IT WORKS...

HERE'S AN EXAMPLE OF A CODE WE'VE CREATED AND IF YOU WERE TO USE THIS, 'HAPPY BIRTHDAY' WOULD BE WRITTEN LIKE THIS:

SZKKB YRIGSWZB

A	B	C	D	E	F	G	H	I	J
Z	Y	X	W	V	U	T	S	R	Q

K	L	M	N	O	P	Q	R	S	T
P	O	N	M	L	K	J	I	H	G

U	V	W	X	Y	Z
F	E	D	C	B	A

WHO'S IN... DANCE CLUB

LINE DANCER

OH HAY!

CHARACTER #: 1-022
CLUB: DANCE
RARITY: POPULAR
SERIES: 1

TRY AND KEEP UP WITH OUR MOVES!

SERIES 1

SIS SWING

DON'T BE A SQUARE

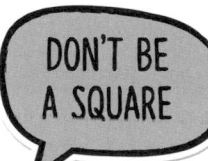

CHARACTER #: 1-023
CLUB: DANCE
RARITY: POPULAR
SERIES: 1

CENTER STAGE

ALWAYS ON POINTE!

CHARACTER #: 1-024
CLUB: DANCE
RARITY: FANCY
SERIES: 1

L.O.L. SURPRISE!

LIL CENTER STAGE

SERIES 1

"TUTU CUTE!"

CHARACTER #: 1-025
CLUB: DANCE
RARITY: ULTRA-RARE
SERIES: 1

WE ALWAYS CLEAR THE DANCE FLOOR!

LIL SISTERS

LIL SIS SWING

"WHEN IN DOUBT, DANCE IT OUT"

CHARACTER #: 2-058
CLUB: DANCE
RARITY: POPULAR
SERIES: 2

SERIES 2

LIL LINE DANCER

"JUST A SMALL TOWN BABY"

CHARACTER #: 2-059
CLUB: DANCE
RARITY: POPULAR
SERIES: 2

GO DANCE CRAZY!

MAKE UP A DANCE ROUTINE WITH FRIENDS, OR COME UP WITH A SUPER SOLO PERFORMANCE!

MUSIC MATTERS

THE FIRST THING YOU NEED TO DECIDE IS WHAT MUSIC TO DANCE TO! THE MUSIC IS JUST AS IMPORTANT AS YOUR DANCE MOVES, SO CHOOSE SOMETHING YOU REALLY LOVE.

WARM UP

NEXT IT'S TIME TO WARM UP THOSE DANCING MUSCLES. YOU DON'T WANT YOUR MOVES TO LOOK STIFF (AND YOU DEFINITELY DON'T WANT TO HURT YOURSELF) SO GENTLY STRETCH YOUR ARMS AND LEGS THEN GIVE THEM A GOOD SHAKE OUT, TOO.

OH HAY! WANNA DANCE?!

STEP BY STEP

LISTEN TO YOUR PIECE OF MUSIC IN SECTIONS AND WRITE DOWN ANY DANCE MOVES THAT COME INTO YOUR HEAD AS YOU GO ALONG. YOU COULD EVEN ASK A FRIEND TO VIDEO THE MOVES YOU COME UP WITH SO YOU DON'T FORGET.

G

ALWAYS ON POINT!

CAN I DANCE WITH YOU? PRETTY PLEASE!

TIME TO DANCE!

ONCE YOU HAVE YOUR DANCE MOVES IN YOUR HEAD, IT'S TIME TO PUT THEM ALL TOGETHER! IT MIGHT TAKE A FEW GOES TO REMEMBER WHICH DANCE MOVES COME NEXT, BUT KEEP PRACTICING AND YOU'LL SOON HAVE A PERFECT ROUTINE.

HAVE A SWINGING TIME AT YOUR SHOW!

THE SHOW

ONCE YOU HAVE YOUR ROUTINE DOWN, YOU MIGHT WANT TO SHOW IT OFF TO YOUR FAMILY AND FRIENDS! ORGANISE A PERFORMANCE IN YOUR LIVING ROOM, GARDEN OR KITCHEN (ANYWHERE THERE IS A CLEAR SPACE TO DANCE).

DON'T BE A SQUARE.

WIN! L.O.L. SURPRISE! GOODIES

ENTER THIS AWESOME COMPETITION TO BE IN WITH THE CHANCE OF WINNING A BUMPER BAG OF L.O.L. SURPRISE! GOODIES. WHO KNOWS WHAT EXCITING THINGS ARE HIDDEN INSIDE?!

HOW TO ENTER...

THERE ARE 8 LETTERS HIDDEN ON SOME OF THE PAGES INSIDE THIS BOOK. ALL YOU NEED TO DO IS FIND ALL THE LETTERS AND REARRANGE THEM TO SPELL THE NAME OF ONE OF THE L.O.L. SURPRISE! DOLLS.

YOU CAN WRITE DOWN THE LETTERS YOU FIND HERE — CAN YOU WORK OUT WHOSE NAME HAS BEEN SCRAMBLED?

EMAIL YOUR ANSWER, ALONG WITH YOUR NAME AND ADDRESS, TO...
BOOKS@LITTLEBROTHERBOOKS.CO.UK

PLEASE ADD THE SUBJECT LINE "L.O.L. SURPRISE COMPETITION 2018".
GOOD LUCK!

© MGA
© MGA
© MGA
© MGA

THE CLOSING DATE FOR ALL ENTRIES IS 31ST JANUARY 2018. FOR FULL TERMS AND CONDITIONS PLEASE SEE PAGE 76.

OFFICIAL 2018 EDITION

WHO'S IN... GLAM CLUB

'A' IS FOR ACCESSORISE!

ROYAL HIGH-NEY

 LE SIGH

CHARACTER #: 1-026
CLUB: GLAM
RARITY: POPULAR
SERIES: 1

SERIES 1

LEADING BABY

 ALWAYS READY FOR MY SELFIE

CHARACTER #: 1-027
CLUB: GLAM
RARITY: FANCY
SERIES: 1

MISS BABY

 PUT A SASH ON IT

CHARACTER #: 1-028
CLUB: GLAM
RARITY: POPULAR
SERIES: 1

 L.O.L. SURPRISE!

IT BABY

"I DON'T DO GLAM, I AM GLAM"

CHARACTER #: 2-014
CLUB: GLAM
RARITY: FANCY
SERIES: 2

© MGA

"OUR NAMES ARE ALWAYS ON THE GUEST LIST!"

SERIES 2

MISS PUNK

"51% PUNK, 49% PRINCESS"

CHARACTER #: 2-015
CLUB: GLAM
RARITY: FANCY
SERIES: 2

DOLLFACE

"FUR-EVER YOUNG"

CHARACTER #: 2-016
CLUB: GLAM
RARITY: POPULAR
SERIES: 2

LIL SISTERS

LIL MISS BABY

SERIES 2

"TIARAS ARE NOT OPTIONAL"

CHARACTER #: 2-060
CLUB: GLAM
RARITY: POPULAR
SERIES: 2

LIL MISS PUNK

SERIES 2

"MY CROWN MAKES ME TALLER"

CHARACTER #: 2-061
CLUB: GLAM
RARITY: FANCY
SERIES: 2

LIL IT BABY

SERIES 2

"TRES CHIC"

CHARACTER #: 2-062
CLUB: GLAM
RARITY: POPULAR
SERIES: 2

LIL DOLLFACE

SERIES 2

"FAUX-REAL"

CHARACTER #: 2-063
CLUB: GLAM
RARITY: POPULAR
SERIES: 2

OFFICIAL 2018 EDITION

IT'S PARTY TIME!

THERE'S NO NEED TO WAIT FOR A BIRTHDAY — YOU CAN THROW A SURPRISE PARTY ANY TIME OF THE YEAR! FOLLOW OUR GUIDE TO PLAN THE PERFECT L.O.L. CELEBRATION.

THINK OF A THEME

THEMED PARTIES ARE LOTS OF FUN AND MAKE YOUR CELEBRATION UNIQUE. CHOOSE SOMETHING THAT CAN BE REFLECTED IN YOUR DECORATIONS, FOOD AND PARTY GAMES. YOU COULD HAVE A GLITTERATI PARTY WHERE EVERYTHING SPARKLES OR A COSPLAY PARTY WHERE EVERYONE COMES DRESSED AS THEIR FAVOURITE L.O.L. DOLL.

INVITE YOUR GUESTS

UNLESS YOU'RE SURPRISING YOUR GUESTS AT THE VERY LAST MINUTE YOU'LL WANT TO SEND OUT INVITATIONS. MAKING THEM YOURSELF ADDS A PERSONAL TOUCH TO YOUR PARTY (SEE THE PAGE OPPOSITE FOR A VIP PARTY INVITATION TEMPLATE).

DECORATE YOUR VENUE

DECORATIONS ADD A WOW FACTOR AND HELP TO BRING YOUR PARTY TO LIFE. REMEMBER TO CHOOSE DECORATIONS THAT TIE IN WITH YOUR THEME. IF YOU'RE HAVING A GLAM PARTY YOU MIGHT CHOOSE TO HAVE A RED CARPET FOR YOUR GUESTS TO WALK DOWN WHEN THEY ARRIVE AND A CHILL OUT PARTY WOULD LOOK GREAT WITH TONS OF BEANBAGS AND CUSHIONS TO LOUNGE ABOUT ON.

PREPARE FOOD AND DRINK

FINGER FOOD IS A GREAT OPTION FOR ANY PARTY. YOUR GUESTS WILL LOVE BEING ABLE TO TRY A LITTLE BIT OF EVERYTHING AND IT'S QUICK TO EAT MEANING YOU WON'T MISS OUT ON VALUABLE DANCING OR PLAYTIME! IT'S FUN TO TIE SOME OF YOUR NIBBLES INTO THE THEME IF YOU CAN. WHY NOT HAVE BLACK AND WHITE SWEETS FOR AN OPPOSITES PARTY OR CUPCAKES DECORATED WITH EDIBLE GLITTER FOR A GLITTERATI BASH?

CHOOSE YOUR ENTERTAINMENT

YOU COULD PLAY PARTY GAMES SUCH AS POP THE GLITTER BALLOONS OR PASS THE PARCEL (SEE PAGES 46 TO 48 FOR IDEAS) OR PLAY MUSIC FOR EVERYONE TO DANCE TO. OR YOU COULD DOUBLE THE FUN WITH A BIT OF BOTH!

VIP PARTY INVITE

USE THIS TEMPLATE TO CREATE PARTY INVITATIONS TO YOUR VERY OWN VIP BASH!

VIP PARTY

TO _____

YOU ARE INVITED TO AN EXCLUSIVE PARTY

ON _____

AT _____

TIME _____

DRESS CODE _____

FROM _____

RSVP

DECORATION IDEAS

- ★ USE GLITTER GLUE TO ADD SPARKLING SWIRLS
- ★ WRITE IN GOLD OR SILVER PEN
- ★ ADD A SEQUIN BORDER
- ★ CUT SILHOUETTE SHAPES FROM BLACK PAPER
- ★ PUT CONFETTI INSIDE THE ENVELOPE FOR AN ADDED SURPRISE!

PHOTOCOPY THE INVITATION AND DECORATE IT TO GIVE TO YOUR FRIENDS. IF YOU DON'T HAVE ACCESS TO A PHOTOCOPIER, TRACE THE INVITATION ONTO PLAIN WHITE PAPER.

OFFICIAL 2018 EDITION

UNWRAP THE SURPRISE!

THE GLAM CLUB ARE ALWAYS SURPRISING EACH OTHER WITH THIS FUN GAME. MAKE IT AND PLAY WITH YOUR FRIENDS!

MAKE THE GAME!

1. FIND YOUR SURPRISE. THIS COULD BE LIP BALM, RINGS, OR A CUTE HAIR BAND.
2. WRAP YOUR SURPRISE IN AN EMPTY L.O.L SURPRISE BALL, THEN COVER IT IN LOTS OF LAYERS OF TISSUE PAPER, WRAPPING PAPER, OR EVEN NEWSPAPER!

MAKE SURE YOU CHOOSE A SURPRISE YOU DON'T MIND GIVING AWAY!

I DON'T DO GLAM, I AM GLAM

LE SIGH

IF YOU WANT TO JOIN IN, ASK A GROWN UP TO DO THE MUSIC FOR YOU!

HOW TO PLAY...

1. SIT IN A CIRCLE AND PASS THE PARCEL AROUND WHILE PLAYING MUSIC.
2. WHEN THE MUSIC STOPS, WHOEVER IS HOLDING THE PARCEL GETS TO UNWRAP A LAYER.
3. WHOEVER UNWRAPS THE SURPRISE IS THE WINNER.

L.O.L. SURPRISE!

SPEED UN-WRAPPER

SOMETIMES UN-WRAPPING THINGS REALLY QUICKLY CAN BE SUPER EXCITING. THE GLAM CLUB ARE ALWAYS LOOKING FOR EXCITING AND FUN PARTY IDEAS, SO THIS GAME IS PERFECT FOR THEM!

FAST AND FURIOUS!

51% PUNK, 49% PRINCESS

HOW TO PLAY...

1. PLACE A SURPRISE PARCEL IN FRONT OF EACH OF YOUR FRIENDS.

2. ALL COUNT "1, 2, 3!" THEN START TO UNWRAP YOUR PARCELS.

3. WHOEVER REACHES THEIR GIFT FIRST IS THE WINNER!

OFFICIAL 2018 EDITION

GLITTERATI SURPRISE POP!

PLAY THIS GAME OUTDOORS SO THAT THE GLITTER CAN BE WASHED AWAY EASILY.

GLITTER QUEEN HAS THE SPARKLIEST, PARTY GAME IN STORE FOR YOU!

WHAT TO DO

1 TAKE A PACK OF BALLOONS AND REMOVE ONE.

2 INSERT A PLASTIC FUNNEL INTO THE NECK OF YOUR CHOSEN BALLOON.

3 CAREFULLY POUR IN SOME GLITTER (ABOUT TWO TABLESPOONS FULL).

4 BLOW UP THE BALLOON USING A BALLOON PUMP. THEN BLOW UP THE REST OF THE BALLOONS FROM THE PACK AND MIX THEM UP. ONE OF YOUR FRIENDS WILL BE IN FOR A SPARKLY SURPRISE!

I GLITTERALLY CAN'T!

© MGA

NEVER BLOW UP YOUR GLITTER BALLOON WITH YOUR MOUTH AS YOU MAY INHALE THE GLITTER! EWW!

© MGA

PARTY PUZZLE!

DUNK ME!

MISS BABY CAN'T DECIDE WHICH PARTY TO GO TO, THEY ALL LOOK LIKE SOOO MUCH FUN. GUIDE HER THROUGH THE MAZE, MAKING CHOICES ALONG THE WAY, TO GET TO THE BEST PARTY IN TOWN.

MISS BABY

© MGA

Feeling energetic?

Yes!

I'm kinda sleepy…

Need cooling down?

Nope, I need to warm up!

Yep, is there a pool around here?

Icy Pops and Ice Cream

What party snack are you feeling?

Cheesy Pizza and Pjs

Cat Donuts

DANCE PARTY

POOL PARTY

SLUMBER PARTY

WHO'S IN... HIP HOP CLUB

LET'S TURN THE VOLUME UP TO MAX!

D.J.

WORK IT B.B.

CHARACTER #: 2-017
CLUB: HIP HOP
RARITY: FANCY
SERIES: 2

SHORTY

SHORTY-LICIOUS FOR YA, BABE!

CHARACTER #: 2-018
CLUB: HIP HOP
RARITY: POPULAR
SERIES: 2

SERIES 2

HONEY BUN

ALL YOU BABY MC'S AINT GOT NOTHIN' ON ME!

CHARACTER #: 2-019
CLUB: HIP HOP
RARITY: POPULAR
SERIES: 2

BEATS

CRAZYSLEEPYCOOL

CHARACTER #: 2-020
CLUB: HIP HOP
RARITY: FANCY
SERIES: 2

 L.O.L. SURPRISE!

LIL D.J.

"SPINNIN' AND GRINNIN'"

CHARACTER #: 2-064

CLUB: HIP HOP

RARITY: FANCY

SERIES: 2

LET ME OUT!

LIL SHORTY

"SHORTY FROM THE TOY BLOCKS"

CHARACTER #: 2-065

CLUB: HIP HOP

RARITY: POPULAR

SERIES: 2

LIL SISTERS

SERIES 2

LIL BEATS

"I DON'T WANT NO NAPS!"

CHARACTER #: 2-066

CLUB: HIP HOP

RARITY: FANCY

SERIES: 2

WE ALWAYS GET THIS PLACE MOVING!

LIL HONEY BUN

"HUG LIFE!"

CHARACTER #: 2-067

CLUB: HIP HOP

RARITY: POPULAR

SERIES: 2

HIP HOP SKILL

WISH YOU COULD BE IN A BAND? ANSWER THESE QUESTIONS AND D.J. WILL LET YOU KNOW YOUR HIP HOP DESTINY!

1. IN CLASS YOU LIKE TO...

A. ANSWER AS MANY QUESTIONS AS YOU CAN.
B. USE YOUR IMAGINATION.
C. HAVE FUN WITH MY FRIENDS.

2. AFTER SCHOOL YOU ALWAYS...

A. GO TO AN AFTER-SCHOOL DRAMA / DANCE / SINGING CLUB.
B. DO A BIT OF HOMEWORK, THEN SPEND TIME ON MY HOBBIES.
C. GO TO A SPORTS CLUB OR HANG OUT WITH PALS.

3. YOUR BEST MATE HAS A PROBLEM. WHAT DO YOU DO?

A. SORT IT OUT FOR HER. YOU'VE GOT HER BACK.
B. MAKE THEM SMILE AND SEE THE FUNNY SIDE.
C. DO SOMETHING TO TAKE HER MIND OFF IT. LIKE BOWLING!

4. YOUR PERFECT LUNCHTIME IS...

A. A QUICK SALAD, THEN A FUN ACTIVITY.
B. QUALITY CHILL OUT TIME.
C. ONE THAT NEVER ENDS!

5. YOU'RE AT BAND REHEARSALS AND THE LIGHTS HAVE GONE OUT. WHAT DO YOU DO?

A. USE A SPOTLIGHT AND BE THE CENTRE OF ATTENTION.
B. CALL SOMEONE TO COME AND FIX IT, WHILE WRITING IN YOUR NOTEBOOK ABOUT HOW IT FEELS.
C. CREEP UP BEHIND YOUR FRIENDS AND MAKE THEM JUMP!

6. WHAT'S THE BEST WAY TO CHILL OUT?

A. FULL ON MAKE-OVER. OBVS.
B. WRITING POETRY OR READING.
C. CHILLING OUT IS BORING. WHO WANTS TO PLAY KURPLUNK?

YOUR HIP HOP DESTINY

Mostly As
LEAD SINGER, RAPPER OR MC

YOU LOVE BEING THE CENTRE OF ATTENTION AND PERFORMING IS YOUR ABSOLUTE DREAM. YOU'RE GREAT AT TALKING IN FRONT OF A CROWD AND CAN DEFINITELY BE RELIED UPON IF SOMETHING GOES WRONG.

Mostly Bs
PRODUCER

YOU LIKE TO BE IN CHARGE, BUT YOU CAN BE A BIT SHY. YOU LOVE MUSIC AND YOU'D BE GREAT AT WRITING SONGS IF YOU PUT YOUR MIND TO IT.

Mostly Cs
TURNTABLES AND BEATS!

YOU'RE A LITTLE BIT OFF THE WALL AND YOU JUST LOVE TO MESS ABOUT! BEING IN A BAND WOULD BE YOUR DREAM, AND THE TURNTABLES JUST LOOK LIKE THE MOST FUN!

WHO'S IN... COSPLAY CLUB

WE ALWAYS DRESS TO IMPRESS!

BON BON

PRETTY IN PASTEL

CHARACTER #: 2-021

CLUB: COSPLAY

RARITY: FANCY

SERIES: 2

FANIME

TEE-HEE

CHARACTER #: 2-022

CLUB: COSPLAY

RARITY: POPULAR

SERIES: 2

SERIES 2

NEON Q.T.

I WANT IT ALL!

CHARACTER #: 2-023

CLUB: COSPLAY

RARITY: POPULAR

SERIES: 2

MIDNIGHT

BLACK IS THE NEW BLACK

CHARACTER #: 2-024

CLUB: COSPLAY

RARITY: POPULAR

SERIES: 2

L.O.L. SURPRISE!™

LIL NEON Q.T.

"STAY BRIGHT"

CHARACTER #: 2-068

CLUB: COSPLAY

RARITY: POPULAR

SERIES: 2

UNBOX ME!

LIL FANIME

"KAWAII!"

CHARACTER #: 2-069

CLUB: COSPLAY

RARITY: POPULAR

SERIES: 2

LIL SISTERS

SERIES 2

LIL MIDNIGHT

"I'M SCARED OF THE DARK"

CHARACTER #: 2-070

CLUB: COSPLAY

RARITY: POPULAR

SERIES: 2

WE LEAD, NOT FOLLOW FASHION!

LIL BON BON

"SWEET!"

CHARACTER #: 2-071

CLUB: COSPLAY

RARITY: FANCY

SERIES: 2

FASHION-FABULOUS!

> PRETTY IN PASTEL

DO YOU LOVE FASHION AS MUCH AS THE GLAM CLUB? HAVE OODLES OF FASHIONISTA FUN BY CREATING A FASHION SHOW OUT OF THE CLOTHES IN YOUR WARDROBE, THEN DESIGN A NEW LOL SURPRISE DOLL OUTFIT, TOO!

> WEAR WHAT YOU LOVE!

SHOW TIME

DELVE INTO YOUR WARDROBE TO CREATE A WHOLE NEW FASHION LINE.

PLAN YOUR OUTFITS

PUT ALL THE CLOTHES YOU WANT TO USE INTO PILES. SEPARATE THEM INTO TOPS, BOTTOMS, SHOES, ACCESSORIES, ETC. THEN DELVE IN TO CREATE FOUR OR FIVE NEW OUTFITS. LAY THEM OUT, READY TO TRY ON.

> I DON'T DO GLAM, I AM GLAM.

> ASK A FRIEND TO BRING THEIR OLD CLOTHES OVER FOR AN EVEN BIGGER FASHION PARTY!

CREATE YOUR CATWALK

A CATWALK CAN BE ANYWHERE YOU HAVE SPACE TO WALK UP AND DOWN. TRY YOUR HALLWAY, LANDING, GARDEN OR EVEN YOUR BED! LINE CUSHIONS ALONG THE SIDE OF YOUR CHOSEN CATWALK FOR YOUR AUDIENCE TO WATCH.

DON'T FORGET THE MUSIC!

EVERY FASHION SHOW NEEDS MUSIC TO WALK TO. CHOOSE YOUR FAVOURITE MUSIC – UPBEAT SONGS WORK THE BEST – AND PLAY THEM WHEN YOU ARE READY IN YOUR FIRST OUTFIT.

REMEMBER: YOU DON'T HAVE TO BE PERFECT TO BE FASHION FORWARD – AS LONG AS YOU HAVE FUN!

PUT ON A FASHION SHOW

DESIGN TIME

USE THE OUTLINE OPPOSITE TO CREATE A BRAND NEW L.O.L. OUTFIT. IT CAN BE ANYTHING YOU LIKE, SO LET YOUR IMAGINATION RUN WILD!

I JUST LOVE WHAT YOU'RE WEARING!

© MGA

OFFICIAL 2018 EDITION

LET'S ACCESSORISE!

THE COSPLAY CLUB LOVE DRESSING UP IN COSTUMES AND ACCESSORIES. JOIN IN THE FUN WITH THESE EASY-TO-MAKE GLITTER SHOES!

YOU WILL NEED...

⭐ A PAIR OF NON-SHINY, FLAT BALLET PUMPS OR ANY OLD SHOES THAT YOU WANT TO ACCESSORISE

⭐ A SMALL PAINTBRUSH

⭐ GLITTER

⭐ PVA GLUE

⭐ A BOWL

HOW TO MAKE...

1. MAKE SURE THAT YOUR PUMPS ARE CLEAN AND DRY AND SPREAD OUT A NEWSPAPER OR A WIPEABLE TABLECLOTH JUST IN CASE THINGS GET MESSY!

2. USE A PAINTBRUSH TO MIX THE GLITTER AND GLUE TOGETHER IN A BOWL — ONE PART GLITTER TO TWO PARTS GLUE.

3. PAINT THE GLITTER GLUE ONTO THE PUMPS IN WHATEVER DESIGN YOU'D LIKE. YOU COULD ADD A SIMPLE SHAPE LIKE A HEART OR CROWN OR YOU COULD JUST PAINT ACROSS THE TOES.

4. LEAVE FOR 10-15 MINUTES UNTIL THE GLUE IS DRY TO TOUCH THEN ADD ANOTHER COAT. KEEP ADDING COATS UNTIL THE GLITTER COMPLETELY COVERS THE AREA WITH NO SHOE SHOWING THROUGH.

5. LEAVE YOUR PUMPS OVERNIGHT UNTIL THE GLUE HAD DRIED COMPLETELY. NOW THEY'RE READY TO WEAR!

L.O.L. SURPRISE!™

ACCESSORISING YOUR SHOES!

YOU COULD ADD GLITTER GLUE TO OTHER ACCESSORIES TOO!

WHO'S IN... STORYBOOK CLUB

OUR IMAGINATIONS SET US FREE!

CURIOUS Q.T.

NEW WORLD. WHO DIS?

CHARACTER #: 2-025
CLUB: STORYBOOK
RARITY: POPULAR
SERIES: 2

HEARTBREAKER

BREAKIN' HEARTS AND TAKIN' NAMES

CHARACTER #: 2-026
CLUB: STORYBOOK
RARITY: POPULAR
SERIES: 2

SERIES 2

HOPS

DOES RUNNING LATE COUNT AS EXERCISE?

CHARACTER #: 2-027
CLUB: STORYBOOK
RARITY: FANCY
SERIES: 2

TROUBLEMAKER

PEAK A BOO

CHARACTER #: 2-028
CLUB: STORYBOOK
RARITY: POPULAR
SERIES: 2

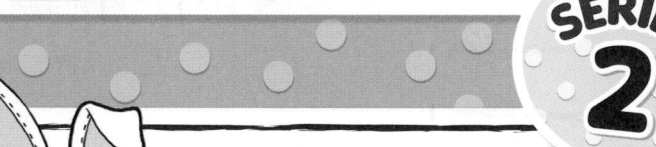

L.O.L. SURPRISE!

LIL CURIOUS Q.T.

"ADVENTURE AWAITS!"

CHARACTER #: 2-072

CLUB: STORYBOOK

RARITY: POPULAR

SERIES: 2

LIL HEARTBREAKER

"FINGERPAINTING THE ROSES RED"

CHARACTER #: 2-073

CLUB: STORYBOOK

RARITY: POPULAR

SERIES: 2

LIL SISTERS

SERIES 2

LIL HOPS

"2 L8"

CHARACTER #: 2-074

CLUB: STORYBOOK

RARITY: FANCY

SERIES: 2

WE ALWAYS HAVE A STORY TO TELL!

LIL TROUBLEMAKER

"HOW'S IT HANGING?"

CHARACTER #: 2-075

CLUB: STORYBOOK

RARITY: POPULAR

SERIES: 2

SURPRISE STORY

FILL IN THE BLANKS TO CREATE A STORY THAT IS TOTALLY YOUR OWN. WHAT WILL HAPPEN AND HOW WILL IT END? IT'S UP TO YOU!

IT WAS THE MONTH OF .... AND HOPS WAS GETTING SUPER EXCITED BECAUSE HER BIRTHDAY WAS JUST A FEW DAYS AWAY. SHE REALLY WANTED .... AS A PRESENT AND HOPED IF SHE WISHED HARD ENOUGH SHE MIGHT JUST GET IT.

WHAT HOPS DIDN'T KNOW WAS THAT HER FRIENDS .... AND .... WERE PLANNING SOMETHING EVEN MORE EXCITING FOR HER — A SURPRISE ....

ON THE MORNING OF HER BIRTHDAY HOPS WAS WOKEN AT THE CRACK OF DAWN BY .... SHE JUMPED OUT OF HER BED AND RACED TO THE WINDOW. SHE WAS AMAZED TO SEE .... OUTSIDE. HOPS FELT .... AS SHE WENT TO TAKE A CLOSER LOOK.

2 L8

If you want a helping hand, use these pictures to inspire your story choices.

HOPS'S FRIENDS HAD PLANNED A WHOLE DAY OF BIRTHDAY SURPRISES. THEY STARTED WITH A YUMMY BREAKFAST OF _____. NEXT THEY ALL PILED INTO _____ AND HEADED TO

_____.

THE FRIENDS HAD AN AWESOME TIME PLAYING PARTY GAMES. _____ WAS HOPS'S FAVOURITE GAME AND SHE DIDN'T EVEN MIND THAT _____ WON INSTEAD OF HER!

THEN IT WAS TIME FOR CAKE. HOPS COULDN'T BELIEVE HER EYES WHEN SHE SAW A HUGE CAKE IN THE SHAPE OF A _____. IT TASTED OF _____ AND _____. DELICIOUS!

THERE WAS ONE MORE SURPRISE IN STORE FOR HOPS. HER FRIENDS BROUGHT OUT A MASSIVE PRESENT WRAPPED IN _____. SHE RIPPED OFF THE WRAPPING AND INSIDE WAS _____.

BEST. BIRTHDAY. EVER!

HOW'S IT HANGING?

WHO'S IN... CHILL OUT CLUB

WE LOVE TO CHILL TOGETHER!

COZY BABE

PUMPKIN SPICE EVERYTHING!

CHARACTER #: 2-029
CLUB: CHILL OUT
RARITY: POPULAR
SERIES: 2

SNOW ANGEL

BRRR...IT'S COLD IN HERE

CHARACTER #: 2-030
CLUB: CHILL OUT
RARITY: FANCY
SERIES: 2

SERIES 2

BRRR B.B.

CHILLIN' WITH MY HOMIES!

CHARACTER #: 2-031
CLUB: CHILL OUT
RARITY: POPULAR
SERIES: 2

POSH

ALWAYS CLASSY AND A LIL SASSY!

CHARACTER #: 2-032
CLUB: CHILL OUT
RARITY: POPULAR
SERIES: 2

L.O.L. SURPRISE!

LIL COZY BABE

"SNUGGLE UP"

CHARACTER #: 2-076

CLUB: CHILL OUT

RARITY: POPULAR

SERIES: 2

LIL SNOW ANGEL

"SNOW BALL FIGHT!"

CHARACTER #: 2-077

CLUB: CHILL OUT

RARITY: FANCY

SERIES: 2

LIL SISTERS

SERIES 2

LIL BRRR B.B.

"IT'S SWEATER WEATHER"

CHARACTER #: 2-078

CLUB: CHILL OUT

RARITY: POPULAR

SERIES: 2

ARE YOU 'COOL' ENOUGH TO JOIN US?

LIL POSH

"SASSY SINCE BIRTH"

CHARACTER #: 2-079

CLUB: CHILL OUT

RARITY: POPULAR

SERIES: 2

SURPRISE CAKE!

BAKE THIS YUMMY CAKE FOR YOUR FRIENDS — THEY'RE IN FOR A SURPRISE WHEN YOU CUT THE FIRST SLICE!

WARNING!

ADULT GUIDANCE IS NEEDED FOR THIS ACTIVITY.

Ⓢ

CAKE INGREDIENTS

- 375G BUTTER
- 375G CASTER SUGAR
- 2 TSPS VANILLA EXTRACT
- 6 LARGE EGGS
- 375G SELF-RAISING FLOUR

(THIS WILL MAKE A THREE LAYER, 8" CAKE)

FLOUR

HOW MANY OF YOUR FRIENDS WILL GUESS THE SURPRISE INGREDIENT?

HOW TO MAKE THE CAKES...

1. PREHEAT THE OVEN TO 180°C (160°C FOR FAN OVENS)/350°F/GAS MARK 4.

2. PUT THE SOFTENED BUTTER AND SUGAR IN A BOWL AND BEAT TOGETHER UNTIL THE MIXTURE IS PALE AND FLUFFY.

3. BEAT IN THE VANILLA EXTRACT.

4. BEAT THE EGGS AND ADD THEM TO THE MIXTURE A LITTLE AT A TIME.

5. ADD THE SIFTED FLOUR AND FOLD INTO THE MIXTURE UNTIL EVERYTHING IS BLENDED.

6. GREASE THE BASES OF THREE 8 INCH CAKE TINS AND LINE WITH BAKING PAPER. SPOON THE MIXTURE INTO THE TINS DIVIDING IT EQUALLY.

7. BAKE IN THE OVEN FOR 25-30 MINUTES. THE CAKES ARE READY WHEN THEY ARE GOLDEN BROWN AND FIRM TO TOUCH.

8. LEAVE THE CAKES TO COOL A LITTLE IN THE TINS BEFORE TRANSFERRING THEM TO A COOLING RACK.

ICING INGREDIENTS

- 300G BUTTER
- 300G ICING SUGAR
- 1 TSP VANILLA EXTRACT
- FOOD COLOURING OF YOUR CHOICE

HOW TO MAKE THE ICING...

1. BEAT THE BUTTER UNTIL SOFT.
2. ADD THE SIFTED ICING SUGAR TO THE BUTTER A LITTLE AT A TIME AND BEAT UNTIL COMPLETELY COMBINED.
3. ADD THE VANILLA EXTRACT AND A FEW DROPS OF FOOD COLOURING AND BEAT WELL.

CAN YOU THINK OF ANY OTHER SURPRISE INGREDIENTS TO ADD?

SURPRISE INGREDIENT!

APPROXIMATELY 150G COLOURFUL SUGAR COATED CHOCOLATE BEANS!

HOW TO ADD THE HIDDEN SURPRISE

1. ONCE THE THREE CAKES ARE COMPLETELY COOL LEVEL THE TOPS USING A SHARP SERRATED KNIFE.
2. USE A LARGE COOKIE CUTTER TO CUT OUT THE CENTRES OF TWO OF THE CAKES TO CREATE TWO CAKE RINGS.
3. ON A PLATE OR CAKE BOARD, SANDWICH THE TWO CAKE RINGS TOGETHER WITH A THICK LAYER OF ICING.
4. FILL THE HOLE IN THE CENTRE OF THE CAKE WITH CHOCOLATE BEANS.
5. COVER THE TOP OF THE CAKE RING WITH A THICK LAYER OF ICING AND PLACE THE REMAINING CAKE ON TOP.
6. USE THE REST OF THE ICING TO COVER THE TOP AND SIDES OF THE CAKE.
7. DECORATE YOUR CAKE WITH PIPED ICING SWIRLS, CHOCOLATE SPRINKLES OR HUNDREDS AND THOUSANDS.

PLAYTIME PUZZLES

IT'S TIME TO HAVE SOME FUN WITH THESE EXCITING L.O.L. SURPRISE! ACTIVITIES...

FIND THE FRIENDS

THE NAMES OF SOME OF YOUR FAVE DOLLS ARE HIDDEN IN THIS WORDSEARCH. CAN YOU SPOT THEM ALL?

NAMES CAN GO UP, DOWN, ACROSS, DIAGONALLY AND BACKWARDS.

HIDDEN SURPRISE! THERE'S AN EXTRA DOLL'S NAME HIDDEN IN THE WORDSEARCH THAT ISN'T ON THE LIST! CAN YOU FIND IT?

```
Y O C X D Z J C H B K E B Z K H L O I Y
X N M R T R C Q E Q X L Q Y F Q L E I Y
A X E X E K B V X N Q J Z K X P C J Y U
Y B A B S S I M I E T M E R B A B Y C I
U V S K S Z C R I Y V E A G Q I H I Z C
A F N G H X K M G K K C R J N C D L I I
S P E A E U R P F L D R E S O S X L Q A
L T E V P G D I N M I S Y N T R U F S C
F C U I Z X A S Y X Q T Y D T A E D F L
U R Q D B Q O T Y F A N C Y U E G T E F
K U R Y X N F L S S F G A E E C R E T A
N M E S U C S U R F E R B A B E M O C E
J A T S W H V R G A X C J Z S T A O J F
R R T V U E U S R B S V G Z H X J I F R
O H I B H E F U U E J F C T V Y O H L E
C P L G Y R J P H L B Z B Z A R R B J S
K T G X A D Y T P M S R C Y M L E Z G H
E U N E H M Z B D Z L V U V B A T U W B
R I L C D I E Z O F F D O S Q A T P Z R
P L C H E E R C A P T A I N A K E H R E
```

♡ GLITTER QUEEN ♡ SURFER BABE ♡ MISS BABY
♡ FRESH ♡ MERBABY ♡ MAJORETTE
♡ CHEER CAPTAIN ♡ CENTER STAGE
♡ ROCKER ♡ DIVA

THE SURPRISE DOLL IS

_ _ _ _ _ _ _ _

SUPERCOOL CROSSWORD

CAN YOU FIT THE NAMES OF THESE CLUBS BELOW INTO THE CROSSWORD? EACH NAME WILL ONLY FIT IN ONE PLACE.

S P I R I T   A

H

T

L

A FEW LETTERS HAVE BEEN ADDED TO GET YOU STARTED!

ANSWERS ON PAGE 76

☆ SPIRIT   ☆ ATHLETIC
☆ OPPOSITES   ☆ DANCE
☆ GLEE   ☆ GLAM
☆ THEATER

WHERE'S SPLASH QUEEN?

ALL OF THE DOLLS ARE ALL HAVING A SUPER TIME AT THEIR ANNUAL DANCE CLUB PARTY, BUT COZY BABE CAN'T FIND SPLASH QUEEN ANYWHERE. CAN YOU FIND HER?

WHO'S IN... RETRO CLUB

'OLD' IS THE NEW, NEW!

JITTERBUG

DON'T WALK DANCE!

CHARACTER #: 2-033
CLUB: RETRO
RARITY: FANCY
SERIES: 2

CHERRY

THAT'S WILD!

CHARACTER #: 2-034
CLUB: RETRO
RARITY: POPULAR
SERIES: 2

SERIES 2

PINK BABY

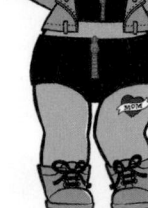

BABY SCHOOL DROPOUT!

CHARACTER #: 2-035
CLUB: RETRO
RARITY: POPULAR
SERIES: 2

B.B. POP

LET ME DO IT!

CHARACTER #: 2-036
CLUB: RETRO
RARITY: POPULAR
SERIES: 2

L.O.L. SURPRISE!

LIL JITTERBUG

"SWING TIME!"

CHARACTER #: 2-080

CLUB: RETRO

RARITY: FANCY

SERIES: 2

LIL PINK BABY

"ON FRIDAYS WE WEAR PINK!"

CHARACTER #: 2-081

CLUB: RETRO

RARITY: POPULAR

SERIES: 2

WE LOVE THAT CLASSIC LOOK!

LIL SISTERS

SERIES 2

LIL CHERRY

"PIN-UP THAT DIPER"

CHARACTER #: 2-082

CLUB: RETRO

RARITY: POPULAR

SERIES: 2

LIL B.B. POP

"I CAN HELP!"

CHARACTER #: 2-083

CLUB: RETRO

RARITY: POPULAR

SERIES: 2

SUPER SURPRISE FORTUNE TELLER

THE RETRO CLUB LOVE FUN, 'OLD SKOOL' GAMES LIKE THIS SWEET FORTUNE TELLER. WHAT SURPRISES LAY IN STORE FOR YOU AND YOUR FRIENDS? FOLLOW JITTERBUG'S INSTRUCTIONS AND UNWRAP THE SURPRISING ANSWERS!

YOU WILL NEED...

- ♥ A LARGE SQUARE PIECE OF PAPER
- ♥ PENCILS OR PENS

SWING TIME!

1 FOLD YOUR SQUARE OF PAPER IN HALF, DIAGONALLY, THEN OPEN IT BACK UP. NOW FOLD IT DIAGONALLY AGAIN, THE OPPOSITE WAY. OPEN IT BACK UP.

2 FOLD EACH CORNER INTO THE MIDDLE OF YOUR PAPER WHERE ALL YOUR FOLD LINES MEET.

3 YOU SHOULD NOW HAVE MADE ANOTHER, SMALLER SQUARE.

L.O.L. SURPRISE!™

④ TURN YOUR SQUARE OVER AND REPEAT STEP TWO, SO THAT ALL THE CORNERS MEET IN THE MIDDLE TO CREATE AN EVEN SMALLER SQUARE

⑤ FOLD YOUR FORTUNE TELLER IN HALF.

⑥ PUT YOUR THUMBS AND FOREFINGERS INTO THE PAPER FLAPS AND GENTLY PUSH UPWARDS TO MAKE THE SHAPE OF YOUR FORTUNE TELLER.

PREPARE YOUR SURPRISES!

ADD A DOT OF COLOUR TO EACH OF THE OUTSIDE SEGMENTS OF YOUR FORTUNE TELLER. THEN WRITE THE NUMBERS 1-4 ON THE INSIDE SEGMENTS. UNDER EACH FLAP WRITE A SILLY, SURPRISE FORTUNE SUCH AS, "YOU WILL BE SUPER-FAMOUS!" OR "YOU'VE GOT A SURPRISE WAITING!"

NOW YOU'RE READY TO SURPRISE YOUR FRIENDS!

HOW TO USE YOUR FORTUNE TELLER...

① KEEP YOUR FORTUNE TELLER CLOSED.

② ASK YOUR FRIEND TO PICK ONE OF THE COLOURS.

③ SPELL OUT THE COLOUR AS YOU MOVE YOUR FORTUNE TELLER IN AND OUT (E.G. FOR RED, MOVE YOUR TELLER IN AND OUT THREE TIMES.)

④ NOW ASK YOUR FRIEND PICK A NUMBER FROM THE INSIDE OF YOUR TELLER, THEN MOVE YOUR TELLER IN AND OUT THAT MANY TIMES.

⑤ TELL YOUR FRIEND TO THINK CAREFULLY ABOUT THE NEXT NUMBER, AS IT WILL REVEAL THEIR FORTUNE!

⑥ OPEN THE FLAP OF THE NUMBER THEY PICKED TO DISCOVER WHAT LIES IN STORE FOR YOUR FRIEND.

PUZZLE ANSWERS

PAGE 68 FIND THE FRIENDS

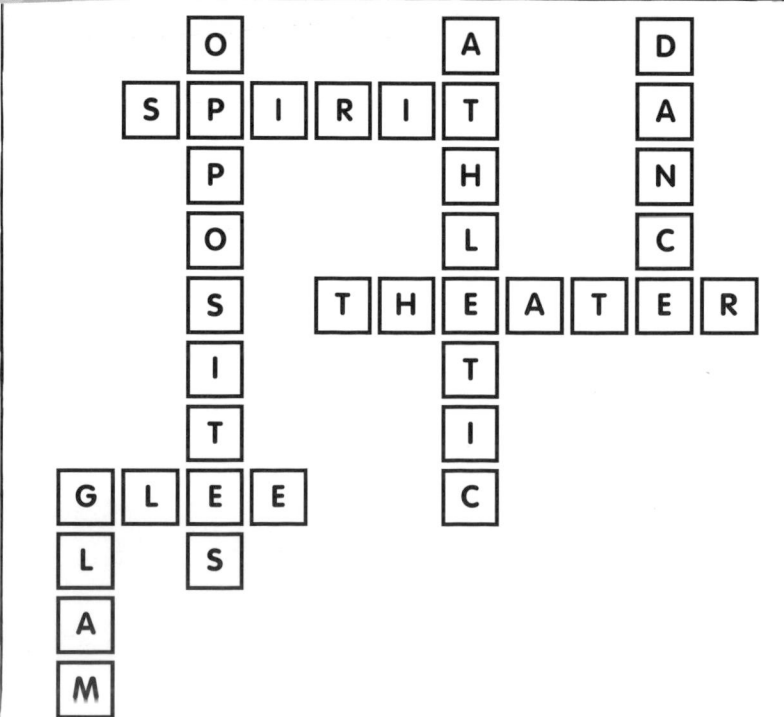

PAGE 70 WHERE'S SPLASH QUEEN

PAGE 69 SUPERCOOL CROSSWORD

COMPETITION TERMS AND CONDITIONS
This competition is open to all L.O.L. Surprise! 2018 Annual readers other than employees of participating companies and their immediate families. Entries are restricted to one per household. Entries must be submitted by an adult (18 years or over) on behalf of a child. We cannot accept responsibility for any entries that are lost or delayed. Proof of sending will not be accepted as proof of receipt. All entries received by the closing date will be entered into a prize draw where the first entrant drawn, with the correct answer, will receive a L.O.L. Surprise! Bumper Surprise Goodie Bag. No cash alternative will be offered. The prize draw will be supervised by an independent person. The editor's decision is final and no correspondence will be entered into.

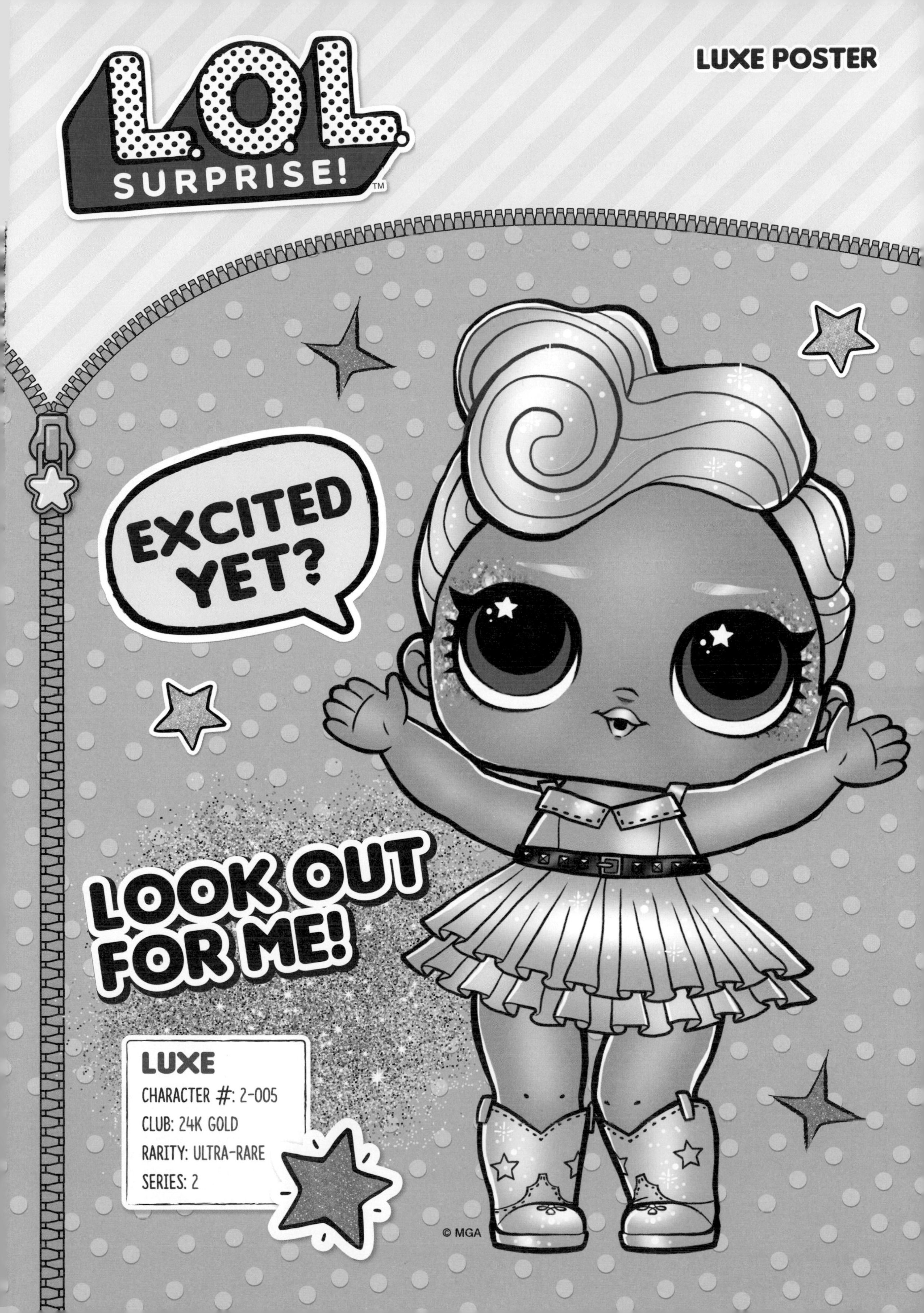

EXCITED YET?

LOOK OUT FOR ME!

LUXE

CHARACTER #: 2-005

CLUB: 24K GOLD

RARITY: ULTRA-RARE

SERIES: 2

© MGA